Cats of Presidents

Grace Hansen

Abdo Kids Junior
is an Imprint of Abdo Kids
abdobooks.com

abdobooks.com

Published by Abdo Kids, a division of ABDO, P.O. Box 398166, Minneapolis, Minnesota 55439.
Copyright © 2022 by Abdo Consulting Group, Inc. International copyrights reserved in all countries.
No part of this book may be reproduced in any form without written permission from the publisher.
Abdo Kids Junior™ is a trademark and logo of Abdo Kids.

Printed in the United States of America, North Mankato, Minnesota.

102021

012022

THIS BOOK CONTAINS
RECYCLED MATERIALS

Photo Credits: Getty Images, Library of Congress, Shutterstock

Production Contributors: Teddy Borth, Jennie Forsberg, Grace Hansen

Design Contributors: Candice Keimig, Pakou Moua

Library of Congress Control Number: 2021939925

Publisher's Cataloging-in-Publication Data

Names: Hansen, Grace, author.

Title: Cats of presidents / by Grace Hansen

Description: Minneapolis, Minnesota : Abdo Kids, 2022 | Series: Pets of presidents | Includes online
resources and index.

Identifiers: ISBN 9781098209247 (lib. bdg.) | ISBN 9781644946893 (pbk.) | ISBN 9781098209940 (ebook)
| ISBN 9781098260309 (Read-to-Me ebook)

Subjects: LCSH: Cats--Juvenile literature. | Pets--Juvenile literature. | Presidents--Juvenile literature. |
Presidents' pets--United States--Juvenile literature.

Classification: DDC 973--dc23

Table of Contents

Cats of Presidents

Almost every US president has had pets. Some have had cats!

Martin Van Buren was gifted a pair of tiger **cubs**. But **Congress** did not let him keep them.

7

Abe Lincoln had two cats.
He loved them. Their names
were Tabby and Dixie.

9

The Hayeses had a cat named Siam. She was the first Siamese cat in the US.

Rutherford
B. Hayes

The McKinleys had an
Angora cat. She had a
litter of four kittens.

13

Roosevelt had a cougar. It was a gift. He gave the cougar to a zoo. He said it would be "properly cared for" there.

Theodore
Roosevelt

The Coolidges had many
animals. Two were lion cubs!

Calvin
Coolidge
17

JFK's family had a cat named
Tom Kitten. JFK was very
allergic to Tom.

18

Socks the cat belonged to the Clintons. Socks' favorite spot was in the Oval Office.

Bill
Clinton
21

More First Pets

Woodrow Wilson
Puffins the cat

Gerald Ford
Shan • Siamese cat

Jimmy Carter
Misty Malarky • Siamese cat

George W. Bush
India • American shorthair

Glossary

allergic

having an allergy. An allergy is a condition in which a person's body has an unusual reaction to certain things, like pet hair and dust.

Congress

the branch of the US government that is elected to make laws.

cub

the young of some mammals.

Index

Visit **abdokids.com** to access crafts, games, videos, and more!